NO LONGER STRANGERS

NO LONGER STRANGERS

Haiku Northwest
Twenty-Fifth Anniversary Anthology

HAIKU NORTHWEST
VANDINA PRESS

Bellevue, Washington

HAIKU NORTHWEST
VANDINA PRESS

Bellevue, Washington

ISBN 978-1-887381-27-7

First printing, April 2014

Copyright © 2014 by Haiku Northwest

Poems set in 13/20 Garamond Premier Pro.
Prose set in 13/20 and 12/17 Garamond Premier Pro.
Headings set in 18/22, 24/28, and 28/32 Veneer Two.

www.haikunorthwest.org

STAFF

Tanya McDonald
Marilyn Sandall
Michelle Schaefer
Angela Terry
Editors

Connie Hutchison
Memorial editor, history, and research

Michael Dylan Welch
*Layout, design, art direction, copyediting,
production, and research*

Dejah Léger
Cover and interior art

Dianne Garcia
Research assistant and manuscript preparation

William Scott Galasso
Publicity and research

ACKNOWLEDGMENTS

THE EDITORS of this anthology are grateful to all past and present members of Haiku Northwest who have so generously offered their poems and their support for this project. They say "it takes a village" and this anthology proves the truth of that adage. We enjoyed reading through submissions from old friends and from new voices, and having the opportunity to highlight both.

As readers might expect of an organization celebrating its twenty-fifth anniversary, a number of our members are now deceased. We wish to acknowledge their important contributions to our community. We are grateful for their families or executors who kindly provided permission to publish their work. Despite our best efforts, we were unable to find family of some of these members; it is our sincere belief that the work of these poets should still be represented in this anthology and we hope that the families agree, should this anthology find its way to their doors.

Thank you again to everyone involved with this publication.

The Editors

CONTENTS

INTRODUCTION

poolside, we chat
about reincarnation;
no longer strangers

—*Francine Porad*

THE YEAR 2013 marked the twenty-fifth anniversary of Haiku Northwest, an active group of haiku enthusiasts in Washington State. In celebration, we have created an anthology that represents the heart of Haiku Northwest. But how do you define the heart of a group that has been active for twenty-five years?

Our founder, Francine Porad, believed that Haiku Northwest should encourage community, poetry, and leadership opportunities. With this anthology, we have tried to honor each of these ideas that form the spirit of Haiku Northwest. This is why you will find no fewer than nine people listed on our production team, filling roles as editors, historian, designer, researchers, publicist, and artist.

Along with sharing the responsibilities of creating this anthology, we wanted our poetry selections to be as inclusive as possible. We sent out a call for submissions to past and present members, including those who were active in the group back when it originally encompassed all of Washington and Oregon. In some cases, this meant using the wonders of the Internet and good old-fashioned sleuthing to track folks down. In other cases, it meant contacting survivors for permission to reprint their loved one's poems. Their work appears in a separate section to honor those poets who are no longer with us. This section also serves to introduce poets who were an important part of Haiku Northwest's past to those of us who never had a chance to meet them.

Another important aspect of Haiku Northwest is its rich history. This history, which has been chronicled by Connie Hutchison, shows how Haiku Northwest began. It also illustrates the group's evolution since 1988 by highlighting key events and projects, as well as some of the people who have been involved over the years.

In continuing with Francine's encouragement of community, the poets in this anthology represent a range of experience levels. Some have been writing haiku for decades; others started writing only recently. Some are well-published poets; others will be able to claim this anthology as their very first publication. Some became involved in Haiku Northwest at the encouragement of friends; others attended their first meeting without knowing anyone in the room. Regardless of how we each came to be a part of this group, we all share a love of reading, writing, and discussing haiku. From past to present, Haiku Northwest's twenty-five years have brought poets together, and we are, as Francine's poem so eloquently states, "no longer strangers."

The Editors

HAIKU, SENRYU, AND HAIBUN

ghost town
and yet an aroma
of fried potatoes

bitter cold
a juniper berry parts
the jay's beak

an'ya
Westfir, Oregon

sunning itself on a river rock her string bikini

in ten summers
the convict's first visit
dragonfly

at the crack of the bat
I lost sight of it;
the full moon

Johnny Baranski
Vancouver, Washington

KALEIDOSCOPE

my routine at the hospice where I volunteer constantly changes. one week I'm hanging out chatting with the residents another I'm doing their bidding. sometimes I just sit in the chapel or at a dying resident's bedside and pray the rosary. today Sister Dominica asks me to go grocery shopping with her. she says she needs me to help her navigate the streets of far Southeast Portland (she's only recently been licensed to drive) and to navigate the aisles of the WINCO food mart a store seemingly ten miles long and five miles wide. what a workout but we get the job done. back at the hospice we stow away the provisions and have a light lunch. later out in the garden a resident asks me to read some of Neruda's love sonnets to her.

knowing death draws near blossoming chrysanthemum

Johnny Baranski
Vancouver, Washington

caked in mud, my feet
stand at the birthplace of kings
honk of a nēnē

we're leaving behind
souvenirs that could curse us
so many more stars

Joshua Beach
Sammamish, Washington

newsprint boat
sinks
from the weight of the news

Gary Blankenship
Bremerton, Washington

writing workshop
her keyboard clicks
enter my poem

night ferry ride
stars brighter
than Ipods

woodgrain of the door
suddenly a forest grove
inside my room

Terran Campbell
Seattle, Washington

Like a wild bamboo
I sleep alongside your travels
waiting for the sound of your feet

Leszek Chudziński
Seattle, Washington

a mottled rock
lifts from the river
    night heron

the teahouse pathway
watered for our arrival
a light rain begins to fall

at a stranger's grave
I rearrange
the plastic flowers

Margaret Chula
Portland, Oregon

IN CASE OF FIRE

After years of traveling in third-world countries, John and I make a point of booking hotel rooms close to the ground floor—and we always check out escape routes. We've read too many head-lines about disasters in poorly built hotels.

At the Las Palmos Hotel in Manila, the first fire escape ends three floors down at a barbed wire gate nine feet high. *Burnt Alive While Trying to Scale Fence!* The second one leads down to the inner courtyard, but first you have to traverse a corrugated roof. When John steps out on it, it starts to give way. *Death by Falling Through Faulty Roof While Trying to Escape Fire.* The third and final fire escape was recommended, even though it's the farthest from our room. The stairs near the bottom are clut-tered with brooms, styrofoam cups, and pipes and metal pieces from construction projects. *Death from Tripping Over a Bucket and Being Knocked Unconscious by an Iron Pipe.* In case of fire, we agree that our best bet is to forget the official fire escapes and dash down the stairs.

I lay out my clothes carefully, untie the laces of my sneak-ers, and hide my valuables under the pillow. For the first time in years, I say a bedtime prayer.

> all night long
> the clang, clang, clang
> of the air conditioner

Margaret Chula
Portland, Oregon

maple tree branches
sprout furry leaf-buds
snow chains back in storage

Nancy Dahlberg
Seattle, Washington

my blue funk . . .
sunlight touches
the distant shore

rainy day
the paper shredder
overheats

Labor Day—
music from the ice cream truck
fades away

Connie Donleycott
Bremerton, Washington

first light—
a fox carries something
through fresh snow

garden pond
a koi nibbles
at spring rain

Agate Beach—
finally finding one
in a gift shop

Michael L. Evans
Shelton, Washington

before me
redwood
after me

food bank line—
striking up a conversation
with my old boss

unrelenting summer—
a termite
tears at its wings

Seren Fargo
Bellingham, Washington

so much to do
my son points out
the lightning

river mint
growing wild—
mid-life

mallard pair
he rocks
on her wake

Alice Frampton
Seabeck, Washington

falling leaves . . .
playing solitaire
at 2 a.m.

cancer diagnosis—
I turn a blind eye
to the weeds

nudged
by ebbtide . . .
Raggedy Ann

Ida Freilinger
Bellevue, Washington

sidewalk café
her love life lousy . . .
now we all know

rain smacks
the hotel's awning . . .
separate cabs

numbers on his arm . . .
a grandchild asks
how he got them

William Scott Galasso
Edmonds, Washington

rising autumn wind
a raven's shadow
breaks apart

his birth-father's name
on the urn . . .
the aspen's shadow

Dianne Garcia
Seattle, Washington

scattered dominoes
new constellations
to argue about

Katherine Grubb Hawkinson
Seattle, Washington

wild strands
blown from an empty nest
I grow my hair long again

water restrictions
the dog digs a dust bowl
in the back yard

Alison Hedlund
Port Townsend, Washington

just a minnow
the granite mountain wobbles
on the lake

three translations
of the same breeze
pine . . . oak . . . cottonwood

almost dawn
cupped in the curve of the moon
the rest of the moon

Christopher Herold
Port Townsend, Washington

at the used bookstore
women I'd like to talk to
books I've never read

Tom C. Hunley
Bowling Green, Kentucky

Needle in the eye
of Noguchi's *Black Sun*
    only from this spot

each stone's mass
pulling the sand raker
into orbit

nap time quiet—
the baby finds lint
between his toes

Connie Hutchison
Kirkland, Washington

NATIVE AMERICAN PRAYER STONE

Earth Sanctuary, Whidbey Island, Washington

We pass cairns and small flags at the entrance. A bullfrog beckons us. Among alders and huckleberry at the bog's edge, a piece of basalt like a mesa. Instructions tied to a nearby branch.

She wavers on one leg while removing her sandals. Barefoot on what was once lava, a time of creation.

Surrounded now by leaf canopy and the shimmer of afternoon sun. Copper and silver coins to one side, a pocket watch, tobacco spilling from a thin wrapper. Silence.

> her necklace
> among the offerings—
> birdsong

Connie Hutchison
Kirkland, Washington

Company dinner,
large plates,
small talk.

June night.
I lie awake
till birds sing

Winifred Jaeger
Kirkland, Washington

under blue lamplight
a leaf falls
into its shadow

with white out
I could wipe you
out of my life

she put on her pink lipstick
& her pink tam &
her redred high-heeled shoes

Beth Jankola
Sechelt, British Columbia

three months pregnant   moon a crescent

two crows perched on a billboard
just over the hill
a speed trap

winter sunlight/a used car dealer

Michael Kettner
Seattle, Washington

a robin sings
outside my window—
i close my laptop

another shot
into the circular file—
revisions

the record player
skips at the end—
mourning doves coo

Roy Kindelberger
Bothell, Washington

the dancers turn a star
in the cedar barn—
winter solstice

sketching the sapling
I will never see grown—
the quiet woods

late start—
my girls retwine the tendrils
of the wind-blown peas

Dejah Léger
Shoreline, Washington

insomnia . . .
wood owls teach me
their love song

intermission—
a fly on the piano
walks a full scale

late afternoon—
the fullness
of the cow's udder

Carole MacRury
Point Roberts, Washington

close enough to touch—
I let the junco lead me
away from its nest

dentist's obituary—
common interests
we could never talk about

rushing stream
my daughter asks to take
the steeper trail

C. R. Manley
Bellevue, Washington

a train passes
toy soldiers tremble
in the sand box

Gerald A. McBreen
Auburn, Washington

top of the Space Needle
how it feels
to spot a whale

fresh gingerbread—
I reread my sister's
coming-out letter

log truck—
an evergreen air freshener
on the rearview mirror

Tanya McDonald
Woodinville, Washington

slow, slow dusk
cicadas flood the pause
between apologies

the doctor says
When you reach our age . . .
All Hallow's Eve

can't be helped the winter moon

Margaret D. McGee
Port Townsend, Washington

a spent leaf
       spindles
on a spider's loose thread

son's fluting whistle
woos the meadowlark
ever   closer

on the back road
crushed clamshells dusting the blue
out of the bluebells

Mary Fran Meer
Bellevue, Washington

hope for world peace—
the sun and moon
of the West and East

Mas Odoi
Everett, Washington

lengthening day
he still returns home
after dark

slanting beams
over the barbed wire fence . . .
her husband on the other side

Nu Quang
Seattle, Washington

one wet morning

the island across the bay

lifts off into mist

Millie Renfrow
Seattle, Washington

mom's house in winter
after the chemo
just her wigs

scenic highway
lined with the reds and golds of
McDonald's

as I sing
the frogs croak
louder

James Rodriguez
Washougal, Washington

last rays of sunlight
savoring the taste
of a salmon berry

starry night:
the Shetland bites into
another apple

the water's surface
broken
a fisherman casts in the rain

Ce Rosenow
Eugene, Oregon

morning mist—
wind shifts
the mountain peak

nest hole
waiting a wren moment
before it reappears

winter apple a hint of vinegar

Marilyn Sandall
Seattle, Washington

tennis backspin
my son asks me
about girls

hospital window
the traffic at both ends
of the day

the big dipper
no matter where I stand
mountain sky

Michelle Schaefer
Bothell, Washington

alone
a cherry petal settles
in the other chair

young fingers run
up and down the keyboard—
baseball glove

spring sunshine—
sound of the windchime's
little glass stars

Judt Shrode
Federal Way, Washington

they bloom again
after the divorce—
black-eyed susans

the shell's story inside the inside

May rain . . .
I stretch my body
over the whole bed

Carmi Soifer
Suquamish, Washington

virginia rail the voice of the mud itself

eroded sandstone   my empty spaces

airplane window
a white line of surf
holds the land at bay

Sheila Sondik
Bellingham, Washington

THE BLUE BRIEFCASE

I was one of the few students who liked Hebrew school. The flame-like letters of the Aleph Bet were keys to a world full of mystery. But most children my age didn't want to spend Tuesday and Thursday afternoons studying an esoteric language with a bearded, ancient-looking instructor.

> spitballs flying
> blackbirds dot
> the power lines

There was much rejoicing in the schoolyard after the last class in June. My father picked me up. We drove home in our usual silence. When we came into the house, I threw my heavy blue plastic briefcase into the air and yelled, "Yay! No more Hebrew school!" It landed with a shockingly loud thud, disgorging its books and papers in front of my startled parents. A stunned silence filled our small house.

> early summer
> the roses not yet blossoming
> with Japanese beetles

Sheila Sondik
Bellingham, Washington

a fist full
of pumpkin seeds
summer slips away

a thousand cuts
the old cherry tree ready for viewing

insects molting in the closet red stiletto heels

Ann Spiers
Vashon Island, Washington

"catch and release only"
the blue heron
takes a chance

through the walls
muffled voices—
my turn next

Gwen Stamm
Eastsound, Washington

into winter's stillness
the cackle-call
of pileated woodpecker

hospice garden,
only thorns
on the rose bushes

Joan D. Stamm
Eastsound, Washington

lapping shore water—
the things we take
for granted

sound of sweeping—
sunbeams appear
between the pines

forgotten words—
we brush eraser bits
off the table

Carmen Sterba
University Place, Washington

pitch black
but for a roadside café
and the Milky Way

long past the hour
the sound of tires
on gravel

before dawn
the Quaker Oats man
a little too cheerful

Dean Summers
Seattle, Washington

Listening to Mozart
the symphony
of your words

M. Anne Sweet
Des Moines, Washington

trying to name
the color of the sun
yellow peony

fast flowing river
no time left
for half truths

our power
to name things
common merganser

Angela Terry
Lake Forest Park, Washington

daffodil blossom
tip just opened holds
one crystal raindrop

frogs cheering
on each
rainy night

Doris Thurston
Port Townsend, Washington

squawking
to please no one
young blue jay

white oleanders
at a backyard picnic—
how young mother looks

Kathleen Tice
Kent, Washington

moving together—
    noise of the bike, silence
        of the dragonfly

Lightning!
stretch of sand between
dark and dark

more than yesterday
the floating peony's red
filling the glass bowl

Richard Tice
Kent, Washington

Garden Shed

On a shaded wall,
tools gather and take on light,
grown handsome with work.

Anne Voegtlen
Bainbridge Island, Washington

hobo camp the moon for a reading lamp

dark moon my escape hatch

wanting her,
not wanting her—
half moon

Karma Tenzing Wangchuk
Port Townsend, Washington

her first report card—
a row of plum trees
beginning to pink

fading light—
I pop a kelp bladder
for my absent son

a change of tides—
the rowboat aground
in a different place

Michael Dylan Welch
Sammamish, Washington

Fresh, vibrant, yawning
Dew heavy blossoms stretch
Waking from deep sleep

Kathleen Whalen
Lake Forest Park, Washington

no wind today—
the cottonwoods
speak in chickadee

the trail narrows—
every shadow
a possible bear

Billie Wilson
Juneau, Alaska

SHADES OF BLUE

gift shops closed—
a low mist
shrouds the glacier

After the last cruise ship of the season casts off and heads into the rainy fog, downtown Juneau pretty much rolls up the sidewalks. A few old standbys—bookshops, coffee shops, the "five and dime store" and others—hang on for the rest of us through the sparse winter months, but there's a ghost town aspect down near the docks.

We rarely visit the glacier during the summer because busloads of tourists don't add much to the ambiance. But we go often the rest of the year—to see what shade of blue the ice might be—or just to take a deep breath and regroup. After a hectic meeting about my client's latest time crunch, and a drive through the boarded-up end of town, I decided a visit to the glacier was in order. But when I arrived, it wasn't there. The same fog that swallowed the cruise ship had claimed the glacier.

Don't get me wrong. I like tourists. Not the pushy, demanding, self-important ones who flash three-carat diamonds and nine-carat tans. But the ones who seem awestruck and grateful just to be in Alaska. I still feel blessed after more than forty years, and I want to hug them as they stand in the middle of South Franklin Street, blocking traffic and pointing toward the mountains.

I try to be a good tourist when we travel, having heard how unwelcome we'd be in some places. Some locals in some locales have grounds for their resentment. They were born there. Their great great great grandparents were born there. I understand and respect that. And I walk softly when I visit their sacred land. But most of us are sojourners, wayfarers. Wherever we live, we've come from somewhere else. And if we feel lucky to be where we are, it's likely others will think so, too, and flock to visit the area we call home.

In some regard, we're all tourists. Chief Seattle, it turns out, may not really have said "the earth does not belong to us; we belong to the earth." Nevertheless, we will forever be drawn to those few unpaved spots on earth that still speak of mystery and awe. They will beckon to us, and they will call upon us to be a little bit more than we might have known we could be.

> coffee break—
> I walk across the skybridge
> just to see some sky

Billie Wilson
Juneau, Alaska

summit
the wind
smokes my pipe

old barn roof
more sky
than shingles

Brad Wolthers
Hillsboro, Oregon

sun blazes the river—
for a moment the swallow
lost in light

gull overhead
the missing feather lets through
a lighter gray

each minnow's shadow
loose on the lake bottom—
only mine attached

Ruth Yarrow
Seattle, Washington

on worn ivory
nicotine fingers
play for the barmaid

at the edge of the Milky Way
he trades his gavel
for clown shoes

we talk on the sofa
becoming a Rorschach
to our friends

Stuart Zobel
Seattle, Washington

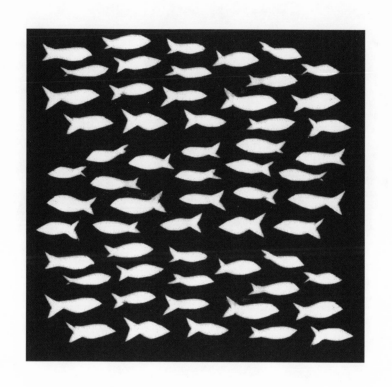

THE INSIDE STORY: HAIKU NORTHWEST'S FIRST TWENTY-FIVE YEARS

by Connie Hutchison

THE HISTORY of Haiku Northwest is one of joy and friendship, making art, learning craft, and creating a community of haiku writers. What's the glue—the factors that influenced our growth and vitality over twenty-five years—and what did we do? What has enabled us to add new members, improve our craft, expand our audience, and explore new directions? Three key elements have made this possible: *personality*, the traits that attract people to the group; *process*, the noncompetitive, positive sharing and critiquing of poems; and *synchronicity*, the dynamic of talented people influencing each other and creating opportunities that benefit the group.

Haiku Northwest was founded by Francine Porad in 1988. Through our mutual friend, Nixeon Handy, I met Francine when she was transitioning from successful painter in oils and aqua media to successful poet, around 1982. The short form of haiku and the quick replies from haiku editors suited Francine perfectly. When she arranged with Alexis Rotella to take over as editor/publisher of *Brussels Sprout*, she asked me to be associate editor. Francine's production of this art and haiku journal, from May 1988 to September 1995, is an important factor of synchronicity for Haiku Northwest. Issues of the journal contain the only written accounts of meetings, guests, and activities of the early group. In these days before the Internet, the telephone and printed flyers were our primary means of spreading the word. Francine also used the journal's "Letter from the Editor" section to announce meeting dates and recap events. *Brussels Sprout* gives us a reflection of the early years until 1993, when Washington and Oregon became the Northwest region of the Haiku Society of America. Ruth Yarrow, who later moved to Seattle from New York, was one of the guest editors of the journal in 1989. With many poets sending Francine haiku and other work, she quickly established herself as a personable and supportive editor. Christopher Herold recounts that his haiku were first published by Francine. For many, meeting Francine was a touchstone for involvement. Here is one of Francine's poems, which so often celebrated human interaction:

> open house
> my children, their children . . .
> joy is my middle name

Haiku Northwest's inaugural meeting took place on September 15, 1988, and is described in the January 1989 issue of *Brussels Sprout*. Guests were British Columbia poets anne mckay, Anna Vakar, and Beth Jankola, and local poets attending were Eve Triem, Sarah Singer, Nixeon Civille Handy, M. Anne Sweet, Connie Hutchison, and editors George Klacsanzky (*Haiku Zasshi Zo*) and Michael Kettner (*Catalyst*). Our Canadian guests each gave a reading, other poets shared their work, and all enjoyed refreshments and a publications display. Beth Jankola's art was later featured in *Brussels Sprout* (September 1999), and Francine and anne mckay wrote linked verse together for several years. This first meeting took place in a building shared by the Bellevue Library and the Bellevue Police Department on Main Street, which has since been replaced by a Lexus dealership.

Regular meetings have been a core factor of our group's cohesion. From 1989 to 1992, they were held every other month in a variety of places, including the Bellevue Library and the Mercer Island Library. Seattle meditational artist Richard Kirsten-Daiensai was a guest in January 1989. He generously brought a packet of his art cards for each person attending. They featured his painting and writing, which he produced during the six months of each year that he lived in Japan in a Buddhist monastery. He was on the University of Washington art faculty and had a gallery in Seattle. His art was featured in *Brussels Sprout* (January 1991). When George Klacsanzky hosted us at his home in the spring of 1989, a dozen poets attended, with special guest Jean Dernberger, the artist featured in *Brussels Sprout* in January of 1989. Again, attendees shared their work, and the group discussed elements of haiku, with good fellowship.

By 1992, our bimonthly meetings shifted to Francine's Mercer Island home, which was decorated with many paintings and art objects, including Francine's work. Francine was a gracious, welcoming host. In this inviting setting, our group learned and honed the craft of writing haiku, shared and supported each other's efforts, and discussed publications where we might send poems. Each person brought a page of haiku with copies so everyone could see the work that we read. We could count on Bob Major to represent a traditional form (three lines in 5-7-5 syllables), while most of us practiced less traditional forms (one to four lines of fewer than seventeen syllables), all concentrating on the *aha!* moment and sensory imagery. Inclusiveness and respect for the spectrum of styles was a principle of our critique—a vital part of our process that demonstrated mutual support.

We commented on what we liked most, sometimes made suggestions, and asked each writer if he or she had any questions about the writing. An early participant, Anne Voegtlen, expressed our process this way: "In our poems and discussions, the group tries to get beyond the cloud of surface facts, to see the deep stillness within the everyday." Awareness of other haiku writers and groups expanded, and we printed "Haiku Northwest Greetings," a haiku sheet, to represent us. It was illustrated with a tree sketch by Francine and featured poems by Carol Edson, William Scott Galasso, Steve Harris, Tom C. Hunley, Connie Hutchison, Mary Fran Meer, Bert Noia, Alice Nelson, Dan Orr, Francine Porad, Sarah Singer, Dean Summers, and Richard Thompson. In 1993, Francine began a two-year term as president of the Haiku Society of America, and Washington and Oregon officially became the HSA's Northwest region, with Mary Fran Meer as its first regional coordinator.

Under Mary Fran's leadership, we had many firsts. The Northwest Region meeting of May 22, 1993, at the Bellevue Library (still on Main Street), featured Paul O. Williams as guest speaker, William Scott Galasso as workshop leader, and a display of books and periodicals. Participants made many new acquaintances. We scheduled monthly readings at North Seattle Community College and at two bookstores: Other Voices in Seattle and Waverly Books in Kent. Beginning in October, we met alternately at the Barnes & Noble bookstore in Bellevue for readings and at Francine's for sharing and critique. In December of 1993, we hosted a national quarterly meeting of the HSA in the spacious new Bellevue Regional Library, where many of our area events have been held ever since. Our featured speaker was vincent tripi, and William Scott Galasso led a workshop. As Haiku Society of America president, Francine Porad was supposed to have chaired this meeting, but unfortunately, Francine dislocated her shoulder when she and another library patron collided. HSA secretary Doris Heitmeyer chaired the meeting, assisted by Mary Fran Meer. Afterwards, many of us visited Francine at Group Health Hospital. In 1994, we published our first regional anthology, *Echoes Across the Cascades*, with original cut-paper art by Carol Edson.

As HSA president, Francine encouraged national and international discourse and friendships among haiku practitioners. These came to fruition in the next decade. Our early meetings with Oregon poets developed into enduring friendships and collaborations. Ce Rosenow and Brad Wolthers accompanied Wilma M. Erwin, the featured speaker at the second regional meeting, held on May 21, 1994 at the Bellevue Library. Jean Dubois from Colorado was the featured reader, Bert Noia led a workshop, and Carol Edson performed. We dubbed October 1994 "Super October." Members read at the dedication of the Yao Japanese Garden at Bellevue Botanical Garden. At the third regional meeting, Margaret Chula gave a reading from her book *Grinding My Ink*, reflecting the years she lived in Japan. In addition, awards for a Washington Poets Association haiku contest, judged by Francine, were presented at the Bellevue Botanical Garden.

Kristin Deming, returning to the United States after living thirteen years in Japan (where Francine met her in 1994), read her poems at the Haiku Society of America quarterly meeting in March of 1998, in Federal Way. We enjoyed a video of her poems set to music and performed at the Imperial Palace in Tokyo. Ruth Yarrow was the featured speaker on "Haiku at Work" and Marc Thompson's workshop posed the question, "If the Way of Poetry is an alternative to the New World Order, then is writing haiku a subversive act?" A performance by Carol Edson, Maris Kundzins, and Munio Makuuchi concluded with participants tossing colorful "aerogami" birds. In January 1999, visiting teacher and poet Kris Kondo led renku workshops at the Kirkland Library and at Francine's home. This was our group's first experience writing together in a linked-verse form. Enthused, we decided to meet *every* month. Tadashi Kondo, a guest at our meeting in February 2000, shared copies of *Wind Arrow*, the 1999 Association of International Renku's anthology in Japanese and English. The twenty-link renku written at that meeting was published in *Chiyo's Corner* in the spring of 2000. We continued to improve our craft and make new connections. Oregon poets Margaret Chula and Ce Rosenow presented workshops to high school students and gave a radio interview and reading in 1999. Margaret Chula, John Hall, and Elizabeth Falconer presented a program of haiku with photos accompanied by koto at the Portland Art Museum. Margaret Chula and Christopher Herold gave a workshop at the Olympia Zen Center in 2000. Several garden walks, regional meetings and the December 2002 HSA quarterly meeting, including workshops and presentations, were coordinated by Ruth Yarrow.

The slam scene also enveloped haiku. Haiku Northwest members have faced other poets in the Seattle Poetry Slam's annual Haiku d'Etat competition at various locations numerous times. At the Sit & Spin tavern and laundry in Seattle, Ruth Yarrow and Bob Major were the finalists one year. Their poems fell into the raunchy spectrum, with Bob winning by audience acclaim. He became the featured reader the next year. Francine was featured in 1999 and Michael Dylan Welch has been the featured reader twice.

Synchronicity is the dynamic of people influencing other people, using their talent to create opportunities that enable the group to grow in experience, skill, and enjoyment of haiku. Our members are talented in many areas such as visual arts, music, photography, teaching, bookbinding, publishing, and networking. Some have become editors and publishers of books and chapbooks, while others have produced periodicals that gave haiku writers the opportunity to see their work in print and to learn from excellent examples. Editors and publishers active in the group's first twenty-five years include Margaret Chula (Katsura Press), Cherie Hunter Day (Sundog Press), Kathleen P. Decker (Laughing CyPress), Wilma Erwin and Brad Wolthers (Mountain Gate Press), Ce Rosenow (Irving Street Press, North Lake Press, Mountains and Rivers Press), Dean Summers (Holly House Productions), and Michael Dylan Welch (Press Here). Some of those who established periodicals in the region include an'ya (*Moonset*), Kathleen P. Decker (*Chiyo's Corner*), Lorraine Ellis Harr (*Dragonfly: A Quarterly of Haiku*—published in Portland, Oregon from 1972 to 1984), Christopher Herold (*The Heron's Nest*), George Klacsanzky (*Haiku Zasshi Zo*—the first haiku journal in the Seattle area, started in 1984, and published until 1988), Francine Porad (*Brussels Sprout*), Edna Purviance (*Portals*—the first haiku-related journal in Washington State, published in Bellingham for three years in the 1970s), Ce Rosenow (*Northwest Literary Forum*), and CarrieAnn Thunell (*Nisqually Delta Review*).

A copy of *The Swinging Grasshopper*, a hand-sewn chapbook, was Bob Major's surprise gift for each of us a month after the August 12, 1995 regional meeting held at the Bellevue Library. This "experiment" contained haiku and haiku-like musings by attendees of the workshop he led using a quote by the Mississippi artist Walter I. Anderson as a prompt. This little Japanese stab-bound book and Bob's experience in the publishing industry, including at the University of

Washington publications department, were the beginning of our development as a group in the area of making hand-bound books. For our regional anthology, *To Find the Words* (2000), edited by Connie Hutchison, Christopher Herold, and Mary Fran Meer, we invited haiku poets in British Columbia and Alaska who share our mountain and ocean landscape to participate. The book was awarded first place in the Haiku Society of America's Merit Book Awards. We issued a second limited edition in 2002 after we learned of the award. In 2008, our cadre of bookbinders partnered with poets from Vashon Island's "Mondays at Three" haiku group to make a chapbook for Helen Russell, our eldest member, for her 99th birthday. We enjoyed a special camaraderie as we sewed with linen thread into handmade paper covers. This chapbook, *Distant Sounds*, won the Merit Book Award for best chapbook published in 2008.

Regional coordinators have played an important role in shaping the group experience. For the Haiku Society of America quarterly meeting at Hugo House in Seattle, organized by Michael Dylan Welch in June of 2008, Connie Hutchison and Marilyn Sandall made collages to honor each coordinator and to illustrate activities during his or her term (photographs of these collages are available on the Haiku Northwest website). These were placed under glass at each table in the room, and have been displayed at several events since Hugo House. Their photos, anthology covers, programs, and other memorabilia remind us of haiku walks we shared in beautiful gardens, anthologies produced and prizes won, readings at bookstores and the Seattle Japanese Garden, beach walks and potlucks at Hood Canal, and performances at the Northwest Folklife festival, Bumbershoot, Aki Matsuri, and other venues. An appendix in this anthology lists all regional coordinators from 1993 to 2013, whose dedicated leadership has contributed to our growth as a haiku community.

Haiku Northwest has been a nucleus for English-language haiku activity in the Puget Sound region, but was not the first haiku group in the area. Lorraine Ellis Harr, writer, teacher and editor, established the Western World Haiku Society in Oregon in 1972. The Washington Poets Association, founded in 1971, published an annual haiku contest anthology from 1975 to 1982. Edna Purviance led the Haiku Appreciation Club in Bellingham (late 1970s) and published books by Betty Drevniok, cofounder of Haiku Canada (1977). George Klacsanzky hosted bimonthly meetings in the Seattle area in the mid-1980s. Since 1992, when Mimi Call and Doris Thurston started the Port Townsend haiku group, other groups have formed: Vashon Island's "Mondays at Three," named for the time they meet, hosted by Helen Russell (1998), the Bellingham Haiku Group, founded by Seren Fargo (2009), and the Mt. Olympus Haiku Society, organized in Sequim by Maggie Jamison (2010). Christopher Herold's publication, *Northwest Haiku Gardens*, produced for one of our many joint meetings, presents haiku from members of these groups. It is a welcome history of the joint meetings that began with Haiku Northwest and the Port Townsend group, and reflects strong ties that developed when the Port Townsend writers made the long drive and ferry crossing to attend meetings at Francine's home. In 2011, Commencement Bay Haiku, founded by Carmen Sterba and Judt Shrode in Tacoma, became the area's newest haiku group.

The 1997 Haiku North America conference in Portland, Oregon, was a milestone. Ce Rosenow (chair), with Margaret Chula and Cherie Hunter Day, gathered an impressive cadre of presenters to explore the theme of innovation in haiku. Highlights included a translation panel with Janine Beichman, Sam Hamill, Patricia Donegan, and Steven D. Carter, moderated by William J. Higginson; a *butoh* performance by Maureen Freehill; workshops on translation with Jerry

Ball, haibun with Rich Youmans, rengay with Garry Gay, Ebba Story, and Cherie Hunter Day, and teaching haiku with Penny Harter and George Swede. We also enjoyed a reading by Lorraine Ellis Harr at the Portland Japanese Garden and a book fair and socializing at the historic Drake Hotel.

Since moving to the Seattle area in 2002, Michael Dylan Welch has widened our horizons and contributed to the synchronicity that is a key factor of Haiku Northwest's cohesion. In our meetings, he expands our understanding of Japanese origins of haiku and its cultural context. He draws others to the haiku arena through his enthusiasm and creates new venues and experiences for sharing haiku. Some of these include establishing the "Haiku Garden" reading series in 2003 at the Seattle Japanese Garden, featuring guest poets and Haiku Northwest members; giving numerous workshops and teaching at schools, parks, and festivals; and organizing major conferences in our area, activities resulting in the addition of many of our recent new members. In 2003, in response to Michael's proposal, the Washington Poets Association established the Francine Porad Award for Haiku to honor Francine's leadership and craft. Michael served as the first judge in 2004, and continued to coordinate, administer, and publicize the contest until 2013 when Haiku Northwest became the sole sponsor.

Wide use of the Internet has changed how we administer contests, submit our work for publication, and publish—on blogs, websites, and social media, unimaginable when Haiku Northwest began. Thousands of people access haiku-related information and photos each month on personal and regional websites. Michael Dylan Welch's website, titled "Graceguts," provides access to authoritative haiku-related material. Michael established the Haiku Northwest website in 2004, the Haiku Northwest Facebook page in 2009, and he maintains both. He also founded National Haiku Writing Month (NaHaiWriMo) in 2010, held each February (the shortest month for the shortest genre of poetry). NaHaiWriMo has more than 1,800 year-round participants on its Facebook page, and it has brought new members to Haiku Northwest and the Haiku Society of America. *The Heron's Nest*, begun by Christopher Herold as a monthly printed periodical, is now a highly regarded quarterly online journal. Tanya McDonald was a savvy facilitator, using email to send periodic announcements to an extensive roster, enabling and expanding our haiku connections.

Fort Worden in Port Townsend, Washington was the site of Haiku North America in September of 2005, another significant event for the region, organized by Michael Dylan Welch, with Christopher Herold, Carol O'Dell, and Doris Thurston. An amazing array of talented poets, translators, scholars, performers, and artists focused on the theme of authenticity. Events included a conversation with Harumi Blyth (daughter of famed haiku translator R. H. Blyth); performances of taiko drumming and *butoh* dance; haibun, tanka, renku, and rengay sessions; presentations by Cheryl Crowley, William J. Higginson, Emiko Miyashita, and Michael O'Connor; teaching haiku with Penny Harter, Lenard D. Moore, Pamela Miller Ness, Bruce Ross, Carmen Sterba, and Dean Summers; haiga, photography, and origami; and readings, including a memorial haiku reading and Ruth Yarrow's haiku about birds with her production of each one's characteristic song. A highlight for many was the chartered boat trip between Seattle and Port Townsend under beautiful blue skies.

In December 2006, the Haiku Society of America voted to recognize the evolution of its Northwest region into two separate regions for the states of Oregon and Washington. For 2007, the new Oregon coordinator was Ce Rosenow and Washington's coordinator was Terran Campbell. At a national quarterly meeting hosted by the Oregon region in June 2007, we once again saw old friends, read at Powell's Books, and met at the Hoyt Arboretum for memorial readings for influential and beloved leaders Lorraine Ellis Harr and Francine Porad, both of whom died in 2006. Building on their legacies, the strong development in each region resulted in more participants, with Oregon and Washington poets holding leadership positions in the Haiku Society of America and other organizations.

Michael Dylan Welch and Alice Frampton cofounded the Seabeck Haiku Getaway in 2008. Michael has been director since its inception, and Alice was the first codirector and registrar, with Tanya McDonald admirably fulfilling these positions from 2009 through 2012, followed by Angela Terry, who took over in 2013. Held annually on Washington's scenic Hood Canal, close to the Olympic Mountains, this long-weekend retreat has attracted attendees from around the country and internationally to enjoy Seabeck's beachfront and forest retreat center each fall. Attendees have been inspired and refreshed by guest speakers, workshops, haiku walks, and family-style meals while renewing and expanding friendships. Guest speakers have included Emiko Miyashita, Penny Harter, Charles Trumbull, John Stevenson, Paul Miller, and Marco Fraticelli. Retreat anthologies of attendees' poems have been produced for most retreats. One of them, *Seeing Stars*, edited by Michael Dylan Welch, won the Haiku Society of America's Kanterman Award for best anthology published in 2009.

"Haiku: The Four Elements," scripted for four readers and musical accompaniment, was a collection of member poems on the themes of earth, air, fire, and water, edited by Michael Dylan Welch. Dejah Léger secured performance spots for Haiku Northwest at two Northwest Folklife festivals. In 2005, we performed "The Four Elements" with Elizabeth Falconer on koto, repeating that performance at Bumbershoot, and at the 2005 Haiku North America conference with instrumentalist James Whetzel. It was also performed at the Seattle Cherry Blossom Festival with James Whetzel and at the Seattle Japanese Garden's Tanabata festival with Silk Strings (koto performers) in 2006. For Folklife in 2008, Dejah sequenced a new collection of poems, "The Sound of Haiku," and accompanied four readers on guitar. Another performance was recorded at Hugo House and later broadcast by KSER radio, and we repeated the performance at Aki Matsuri, also in 2008.

Under the leadership of our most recent coordinators, Michael Dylan Welch, Tanya McDonald, and Katharine Hawkinson, members have staffed tables and given workshops at Bellevue College's popular Aki Matsuri Japanese festival, Sakura-Con, and the Skagit River Poetry Festival. For the Nature Consortium's Arts in Nature festival in 2010, "Haiku on Sticks" were created pairing the Haiku Northwest logo, designed in 2008 by Susan K. Miller, with members' haiku. These were placed around Camp Long for families to discover throughout the wooded area. Katharine Hawkinson organized the February 2012 HSA quarterly meeting. HSA president Ce Rosenow attended, scholar Richard Tice shared insights about haiku, and Michael Dylan Welch talked about National Haiku Writing Month (NaHaiWriMo). Teruko Kumei presented a paper, "Evolution of American Senryu," which discussed work by Yakima-area residents who, around 1911, established the first Japanese-language senryu group known to exist in the United States. From our library meeting room we posted information about our event on Facebook as it was unfolding and enjoyed being able to share our event so quickly with others interested in haiku.

Seattle-area members have facilitated programs and sponsored innovative events that highlight the interrelationship of haiku and other artistic ventures. For the Haiku Foundation's National Haiku Day on April 17, 2011, Tracy Koretsky and Dianne Garcia organized an art and poetry event. At Seabeck 2012, the Puget Sound Sumi Artists taught a workshop, shared haiga, and graciously participated in the anthology *Windfall*. They also displayed recent haiga at the June 2013 national quarterly meeting at the Wing Luke Museum of the Asian Pacific Experience in Seattle. We were encouraged to "Write like Issa" (HSA president David Lanoue), and to sketch "small scenes from a larger life" (novelist David Patneaude). We learned about the translation of haiku from Japanese (Jeff Robbins, Bashō researcher, visiting from Japan), and HSA vice president Michael Dylan Welch presented a multimedia retrospective of Francine Porad's art and poetry, "Haiku Joy." We also read poems selected for this anthology, *No Longer Strangers*.

The August 2011 Haiku North America conference was the third held in the Pacific Northwest. This event has been held more times in our area than in any other region of the continent. The 2011 theme was "Fifty Years of Haiku," relating to the fiftieth anniversary of Seattle Center and the Space Needle, completed for the 1962 World's Fair. The conference was directed by Michael Dylan Welch, working with Tanya McDonald, Dejah Léger, and Angela Terry, and with key volunteers Dianne Garcia, Katharine Hawkinson, and Tracy Koretsky. More than a hundred attendees at Seattle Center were inspired by workshops, readings, the bookfair, haiga displays, panel discussions, presentations, and excursions to Seattle attractions, including a haiku walk to the Olympic Sculpture Park, a monorail trip to Pike Place Market and the Seattle Art Museum, and a boat trip to Blake Island and Tillicum Village, organized by Katharine Hawkinson. The Higginson Memorial Lecture was delivered by Richard Gilbert. Charles Trumbull and Terry Ann Carter presented histories of haiku in the United States and Canada, respectively. Cor van den Heuvel was the featured haibun reader and Marjorie Buettner delivered the memorial reading. A variety of haiku-related forms were addressed: one-liners (Jim Kacian), concrete poems (Carlos Colón), gendai (Paul Miller, Michael Dylan Welch), rengay (Garry Gay), haibun (Penny Harter), video renku (Eve Luckring), blogging (Ce Rosenow), spaciousness in haiku (Bruce Ross), and food *kigo* with a tasting session (Emiko Miyashita). One particularly popular event was Jim Kacian's coordination of the "Haiku Bowl" quiz show, with trivia questions relating to haiku and its history. At the Space Needle banquet, Haiku Elvis made a special appearance, to everyone's delight. Conference days began with tai chi and haiku led by Don Baird and culminated Saturday night with an exuberant contra dance to music by La Famille Léger.

Though we find ourselves increasingly using electronic media, we continue our tradition of monthly meetings in public settings and in private homes. When the Bellevue Library closed its meeting rooms for remodeling, we met monthly at Lake Forest Park, and this new location attracted new members. When the Bellevue Library was otherwise unavailable for meetings, especially during tax season, members hosted meetings or events in the ambience of their homes.

Margaret Chula and Ce Rosenow (in Oregon) and Christopher Herold, Michael Dylan Welch, and Ruth Yarrow (in Washington) deserve special note for their extensive contributions to the understanding and visibility of haiku in this region and beyond. Their writing practice, research, publications, teaching, workshop presentations, and public speaking have made a broad audience aware of this art form, strengthened the craft and connections among haiku writers, and promoted cross-cultural appreciation and understanding. I think of them as ambassadors of haiku. Their unique combinations of personality, attention to process, and synchronicity continue to vitalize and enrich not only Haiku Northwest, but also the greater haiku community, and we are grateful.

With an analogy, I wish to emphasize the contribution of Helen Russell to the writing of haiku in our region. A pink dogwood has been growing in my yard for three decades. Last year, a robin built a nest in its branches, transforming the old tree into something more—something deeply mature. Similarly, the death poem (*jisei*) of our beloved member, Helen Russell, deepens our perspective. We have had, to my knowledge, no *jisei* from other poets in our region. In her last hour at age 101, Helen dictated her poem to a nurse who had moved the furniture so Helen could enjoy the view:

> first night in new digs
> arranging furniture
> I no longer have

Ann Spiers describes this poem as Helen's last gift to us. Helen joined an elite circle of *jisei* writers, one usually associated with Japanese haiku masters. I admire her focus and clarity as death became imminent. While we continue to support each other in writing and sharing haiku, we too can aspire to such mindfulness and dedication.

Since we were first inspired by founder Francine Porad's leadership, generosity, and innovation, many individuals have contributed to building the community we call Haiku Northwest. We are grateful for their involvement. Haiku Northwest has been remembered in the will of Jay Gelzer and we are thankful for the new opportunities this gracious bequest will make possible. We have flourished and matured in these twenty-five years and are confident that the art of haiku-writing and congenial, supportive relationships will continue for many years to come.

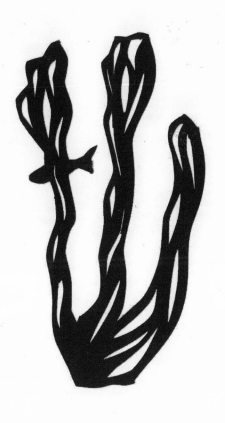

HAIKU NORTHWEST POETS:
IN MEMORIAM

carrying firewood
to the house—
winter in every breath

breath barely visible—
under the dawn moon
white mushrooms

Nasira Alma (1943–1997)

sunflower fading
a shower of gold falls
on the leaf below

Costa Rica
at midnight, you can hear
the earth breathing

Mimi Call (1920–2011)

darkening path
the white morning glories
lead the way

full spring moon—
we can't stop dancing
on the tennis court

Wilma M. Erwin (1936–1995)

twilight
the crows outlast
the gardener

across the room
we smile
the same smile

Jay Gelzer (1943–2012)

sometimes

after   in the emptiness

nirvana

porch swing

  now and then   a breeze

    from the river

Robert Gibson (1923–2003)

salt of tears

on the tongue

no answers

Nixeon Civille Handy (1909–2002)

an owl hoots darkness down from the hollow oak

The sparkler goes out
and with it—the face
of the child.

Lorraine Ellis Harr (1912–2006)

on the wet sand
bird print calligraphy
   flourishes of seaweed

dusk on the lake
 fish keep jumping
  where we were

Helen Ronan Jameson (1922–2002)

empty elevator
one purple
sock

dead loon on the beach
its head nods as each wave
comes and goes

George Klacsanzky (1956–2003)

Soft greens
And cherries full bloom
But peace?

Elizabeth Kusuda (1924–2009)

Among the great stones
set to defend the castle . . .
young ferns take refuge

silent Friends meeting . . .
the sound of chairs being moved
to enlarge the circle

Robert Major (1920–2008)

Ah! spring comes
blades of grass, poems, and ourselves
grow of themselves

Munio Makuuchi (1934–2000)

pale fingers
polishing her days

        a scent of lemon lingering

and the pears we waited for . . .
ripening too late

        by a too thin sun

anne mckay (1932–2003)

Lily pads float
cradled in water
on the edge of air

Lilacs swaying
on the early morning breeze
the taste of purple

John L. Platt (1925–2001)

vacation's end:
I learn by heart
the cloudless blue

bird house empty of seed
even the jays
look for Bernard

Francine Porad (1929–2006)

he tells me the word
I'm looking for
total eclipse

a cloud across the sun
and suddenly
I am old

Helen Russell (1909–2011)

After the blind
Amnesty of sleep
Light so bright it clatters

Wind a muted horn
In the uncertain light
Swirl of leaves

Sarah Singer (1915–2011)

In the tasseling
   corn
fireflies
      swap light

two birds eat and eat
   a withered fruit; far above
   a bird is singing

Eve Triem (1902–1992)

daylight moon—
the pregnant moose
settles into snow

woodpecker—
the silence when my shadow
touches the tree

Cindy Zackowitz (1965–2012)

APPENDIXES

HAIKU NORTHWEST COORDINATORS

Northwest Region (Oregon and Washington),
Haiku Society of America, 1993–2006
Washington Region, Haiku Society of America, 2007–2013

1993–1994	Mary Fran Meer
1995–1996	Robert Major
1997	Cherie Hunter Day
1998–2000	Connie Hutchison
2001–2002	Ruth Yarrow
2003	Carol O'Dell
2004–2005	Marilyn Sandall
2006–2007	Terran Campbell
2008–2009	Michael Dylan Welch
2010–2011	Tanya McDonald
2012	Katharine Hawkinson
2013	Tanya McDonald

HAIKU NORTHWEST PUBLICATIONS

The following is a list of all Haiku Northwest and Northwest Region anthologies, haiku sheets, and related group publications.

1992   *Haiku Sheet #1*, editors: Francine Porad, Connie Hutchison; art: Francine Porad.

1994   *Echoes Across the Cascades*, editorial committee: Connie Hutchison, Robert Major, Mary Fran Meer; typography and design: Francine Porad; art: Carol Edson.

1995   *The Swinging Grasshopper*, anthology of poems by workshop attendees, written to a prompt given by regional coordinator Robert Major at the second regional meeting, August 12, 1995, edited and hand-bound (Japanese stab-binding technique) by Robert Major.

1995   *Sudden Shower*, editorial and design committee: Carol Edson, Randal Johnson (anthology editor), Marilyn Sandall; typography: Francine Porad; art: Carol Edson.

1996   *Unbroken Curve*, editor: Cherie Hunter Day; associate editor: Ce Rosenow; haiku judges: John Budan, Margaret Chula, Ce Rosenow; layout and design: Cherie Hunter Day, Ce Rosenow; art: Cherie Hunter Day.

1996/1997   *Sunlight Through Rain: A Northwest Haiku Year*, editors: Robert Major, Francine Porad; typography and design: Francine Porad; illustrations: Doris Thurston; sequencing: Connie Hutchison.

1997   *Cherry Blossom Rain*, editor: Mary Fran Meer; associate editors: Dean Summers, Marc Thompson; art: Lidia Rozmus.

2000   *To Find the Words*, editors: Connie Hutchison, Christopher Herold, Mary Fran Meer; design committee: Francine Porad, Robert Major, Peggy Olafson, Dean Summers; typography: Peggy Olafson; art: Francine Porad; hand binding by area members. This hand-bound limited edition of 85 copies was awarded the Haiku Society of America's first place Merit Book Award in 2001.

2001   *Sand Water Sky: A Ginko at Alki Beach*, editor, photo art, production: Marilyn Sandall; sequencing: Connie Hutchison; layout: Coryl Celene-Martel; production: Lucy Hart; an 11 x 17-inch paper cut and folded into thirty facets, 2.75 x 4.25 inches, with rice paper over board covers. The book opens from four different directions.

2001   *On Crimson Wings: Centennial Anthology of the Japanese Consulate of Seattle*, Redmond, Washington: Laughing CyPress, editors: Kathleen Decker, Francine Porad, Dean Summers, Kuniko Takamura; sequencing: Connie Hutchison; art: Kathleen Decker, Francine Porad, Aki Sogabe, Teiko Shimazaki.

2002   *To Find the Words*, second limited edition of 86 copies, covers affixed with Merit Book Award seal for 2000;

editing and production by the same members who were involved with the original book in 2000.

2002   *Illustrated Haiku Sheet: Ginko of Northwest Poets at Bellevue Botanical Garden*, April 21, 2002; production and illustration: Ruth Yarrow.

2002   *Box Anthology*, designed by Francine Porad and Marilyn Sandall for December 2002 national Haiku Society of America meeting: loose haiku cards decorated by each author and collected in a covered box.

2004   *Wind Shows Itself*, editorial committee: Francine Porad, Mary Fran Meer, Larry Hussey, Marilyn Sandall; typography: Francine Porad; sequencing: Connie Hutchison; art: Carol Blackbird Edson; 4.25 x 5.5-inch book bound with Japanese stab binding.

2005   *Haiku Sheet with Photos*, Boedel Reserve Ginko, June 5, 2005; production and photography by Marilyn Sandall.

2005   *Haiku: The Four Elements*, folded, one-page program; a sampling of Haiku Northwest members' poems on the subjects of earth, air, fire, and water, edited by Michael Dylan Welch, performed at Bumbershoot on September 5, 2005, accompanied by Elizabeth Falconer on koto; also reprinted for a performance at the Haiku North America conference in Port Townsend, Washington on September 24, 2005 with musical accompaniment by James Whetzel.

2008   *Spring Fever*, a trifold collection of haiku from members of the Port Townsend haiku group performed by Haiku Northwest's David Ash, playing wooden flute, with Marilyn Sandall and William Scott Galasso reading, at the May 10, 2008 joint meeting of both groups in Bellevue, Washington.

2008   *Branching Trails*, trifold edited by Christopher Herold for the November 8, 2008 joint meeting at Doris Thurston's home in Port Townsend; Haiku Northwest poems performed by Port Townsend group members accompanied by marimba, tablas, piano, clarinet, and percussion instruments.

2008   *Distant Sounds*, poems of Helen Russell, editors: Connie Hutchison, Ann Spiers, Ruth Yarrow; design and layout: Connie Hutchison; production: Connie Hutchison, Ann Spiers, Ruth Yarrow, and members of Haiku Northwest and Vashon Island's Mondays at Three group; this book was created to honor Helen's 99th birthday, hand-sewn using Japanese stab binding with black linen thread into covers of handmade mulberry paper, with Thai marbled endsheets; awarded the Kanterman Award from the Haiku Society of America for best chapbook in 2009.

2009   *Feathering the Moment: A Haiku Appreciation Exercise,* Port Townsend, Washington: privately published. Christopher Herold led a workshop at Seabeck in 2008 in which participants contributed phrases found "in this place at this time." Christopher sent all phrases to each participant who linked two phrases in haiku form, resubmitting haiku to Christopher who published this anthology of these collaborative haiku, none of which are the sole property of any one participant.

2009   *Hatku*, edited by Christopher Herold; a four-page pamphlet presenting haiku about hats, written by attendees for the third joint meeting of Haiku Northwest and the Port Townsend haiku group, July 11, 2009, on Marrowstone Island.

2009   *The Capping of the Wild Hatku*, tan-renga edited by Christopher Herold; a four-page pamphlet containing the collection of *Hatku* poems shared at the July 11, 2009 joint meeting, with additional two-line capping verses written in response to each haiku, accompanied by an insert describing tan-renga.

2009   *Woolly Bears & Cedar Flashing*, Seabeck Haiku Getaway anthology; editor: Tanya McDonald; design and layout: Tanya McDonald; production: Tanya McDonald and Michael Dylan Welch; hand-sewn binding of butterscotch-colored covers with iridescent copper end sheets.

2009   *Seeing Stars*, Seabeck Haiku Getaway anthology; editor: Michael Dylan Welch; design and layout: Michael Dylan Welch; production: Tanya McDonald and Michael Dylan Welch; galactiku and other star-related poems written in response to Penny Harter's workshop using images taken by the Hubble Space Telescope; charcoal text papers hand-sewn binding of printed covers with iridescent black endsheets; awarded the Kanterman Award from the Haiku Society of America for best anthology in 2010.

2009   *Seabeck Tan-Renga*, editors: Christopher Herold, Penny Harter, Karma Tenzing Wangchuk; commentary by Christopher Herold; tan-renga written by retreat attendees at the 2009 Seabeck tan-renga workshop.

2010   *From Leaf to Leaf*, Seabeck Haiku Getaway anthology (published in 2011); editors: Tanya McDonald and Michael Dylan Welch; illustrations: Dorothy Matthews; layout and design: Michael Dylan Welch, production: Susan Callan; hand-sewn binding of 4.5x11-inch russet-colored cover with marbled paper accents.

2010   *Keepers of the Light*, editor: Christopher Herold, Port Townsend, Washington: Kanshiketsu Press; a limited-edition chapbook to commemorate the sixth joint meeting of the various haiku groups in Washington State, held October 2, 2010 at Point Wilson Lighthouse in Port Townsend, Washington.

2011   *Northwest Haiku Gardens*, editor: Christopher Herold, Port Townsend, Washington: Kanshiketsu Press; a limited-edition chapbook to commemorate the seventh joint meeting of the various haiku groups in

Washington State, including a comprehensive description of all joint meetings of Haiku Northwest with other haiku groups in Washington State.

2011   *Bound by the Beauty*, Seabeck Haiku Getaway anthology; design and production: Michael Dylan Welch; a holograph anthology with poems by attendees, handwritten and decorated on multicolored cards, collected in a custom-labeled box.

2012   *Windfall*, Seabeck Haiku Getaway anthology; editors: Connie Hutchison and Ruth Yarrow; layout: Dianne Garcia; book design: Connie Hutchison; sumi-e: Fumiko Kimura and Frank Kawasaki; photography: Nick Felkey and Michael Dylan Welch; production: Dianne Garcia, Connie Hutchison, Ruth Yarrow, and members of Haiku Northwest; hand-bound with bamboo and waxed linen into handmade mulberry paper covers, with fold-out pages for art and group photo.

2013   *A Warm Welcome*, Seabeck Haiku Getaway anthology (published in 2014); editors: Michael Dylan Welch and Angela Terry; artwork: Annette Makino.

CONTRIBUTOR PUBLICATION CREDITS AND AWARDS

Many contributions to this anthology were first or previously published where indicated. Our grateful thanks for permission to reprint this work. Works not listed here are previously unpublished.

Nasira Alma: "carrying firewood to the house" *Frogpond* 20:3, December 1997. "breath barely visible" Editors' Choice *Brussels Sprout* XI:2, May 1994.

an'ya: "ghost town" First Prize, Kaji Aso Studio Contest, 2001. "bitter cold" *Heron's Nest* Double Grand Prize Volume 2: 2000.

Johnny Baranski: "at the crack of the bat" and "sunning itself" *Modern Haiku*, 43.2, Summer 2012. "in ten summers" *Heron's Nest* XIII:4, December 2011. "Kaleidoscope" *Haibun Today* Volume 6, Number 4, December 2012.

Terran Campbell: "woodgrain of the floor" *Standing Still*, Haiku North America Conference Anthology, Michael Dylan Welch and Ruth Yarrow, editors. Sammamish, Washington: Press Here, 2011.

Wilma M. Erwin: "darkening path" Museum of Haiku Literature (Tokyo) Award, *Frogpond* 15:2, Fall–Winter 1992.

Michael L. Evans: "first light" Award, Basho's 360th Anniversary Web Haiku Contest. Japan: 2004. "garden pond" *Heron's Nest* 5:7, July 2002. "Agate Beach" Second Place, 2001 San Francisco International Senryu Contest, and in *Pegging the Wind: Red Moon anthology*, Jim Kacian et al, editors. Winchester, Virginia: Red Moon Press, 2002.

Seren Fargo: "before me" *Modern Haiku*, 43.3, Fall 2012. "food bank line" *Haiku News* 1:3. *Lyrical Passion Poetry E-Zine*, 2012–2013. "unrelenting summer" 2011 Francine Porad Contest, Second Place, Haiku Northwest website.

Alice Frampton: "so much to do" *Haiku Canada Newsletter* Volume 14, June 2001. "river mint" Mann Library Haiku Website, February 2010. "mallard pair" Honorable Mention, Henderson Haiku Contest, 2006.

Ida Frelinger: "falling leaves" *Modern Haiku*, 43:2, Summer 2012.

William Scott Galasso: "sidewalk café" *Paper Wasp* 17:1, Summer 2011. "rain smacks" *South by Southeast* XVIII:1, 2011. "numbers on his arm" *Standing Still*, Haiku North America Conference Anthology, Michael Dylan Welch and Ruth Yarrow, editors. Sammamish, Washington: Press Here, 2011.

Dianne Garcia: "rising autumn wind" *Modern Haiku* 43:3, Fall 2012. "birth-father's name" *Sharing the Sun* Members' Anthology, Scott Mason, editor. Chappaqua, New York: Haiku Society of America, 2010.

Robert Gibson: "sometimes" *Frogpond* 20:3, December 1997. "porch swing" Museum of Haiku Literature Award, *Frogpond* 20:2, September 1997.

Nixeon Civille Handy: "salt of tears" *Brussels Sprout* VII:1, January 1990.

Lorraine Ellis Harr: "an owl hoots" *Cicada* 2:3, 1978. "The sparkler goes out" *Dragonfly* 2:3, 1973.

Katherine Grubb Hawkinson: "scattered dominos" *Standing Still*, Haiku North America Conference Anthology, Michael Dylan Welch and Ruth Yarrow, editors. Sammamish, Washington: Press Here, 2011.

Alison Hedlund: "wild strands" *Tinywords*, March 2013.

Christopher Herold: "just a minnow" *Woodnotes* #31 and the Herb Barrett Award (2000). "three translations" *A Path in the Garden*, Portland, Oregon: Katsura Press 2000. "almost dawn" First Place, San Francisco International Haiku Contest, 1999.

Connie Hutchison: "Needle in the eye" *Fleeting Beauty* limited edition chapbook, 2012, Ann Spiers, editor. "each stone's mass" *Wind Shows Itself,* Haiku Northwest Anthology. Mercer Island, Washington: Vandina Press, 2004

Winifred Jaeger: "Company dinner" *Cherry Blossom Rain,* Northwest Region Anthology, Bellevue, Washington: Northwest Region, Haiku Society of America, 1997. "June night" *Sunlight Through Rain: A Northwest Haiku Year,* Northwest Region Anthology, Mercer Island, Washington: Vandina Press, 1996.

Helen Ronan Jameson: "on the wet sand" Editors' Choice, *Brussels Sprout* XII:2, May 1995.

Beth Jankola: "under blue lamplight" *Raw Nervz* 1:2, Summer 1994. "with white out" and "she put on her pink lipstick" *Raw Nervz* V:4, Winter 1998–1999.

Michael Kettner: "three months" *Brussels Sprout* X:1, January 1993. "two crows perched" *Spin,* Winter 1996. "winter sunlight" *Frogpond* 19:3, December 1996.

George Klacsanzky: "empty elevator" *Brussels Sprout* V:2, September 1988. "dead loon on the beach" *Brussels Sprout* XII:3, September 1995.

Dejah Léger: "the dancers turn a star" *Acorn,* #26, Spring 2011. "sketching a sapling" 2013 Francine Porad Award, *Windfall,* Connie Hutchison and Ruth Yarrow, editors. Bellevue, Washington: Haiku Northwest, 2012.

Carole MacRury: "insomnia" *Samobor 20th Anniversary Anthology,* Đurđa Vukelić Rožić, editor. Samobor, Croatia, 2012. "intermission" Honorable Mention, 2009 Betty Drevniok Award. "late afternoon" Merit Award, *World Haiku Review* Fourth Annual Kukai, *Rain Song,* Haiku Canada Members' Anthology, Ottawa, Ontario: Haiku Canada, 2006.

Robert Major: "Among the great stones" Second Place, 1999 Kusamaku-ra Haiku Contest. "silent Friends meeting" *Heron's Nest* 4:8, August 2002.

Munio Makuuchi: "Ah! spring comes" *The Swinging Grasshopper*, work-shop anthology, August 1995, Robert Major, editor.

C. R. Manley: "close enough to touch" Third Place, 2009Henderson Haiku Contest, *Frogpond*, 33:1, Winter 2010. "dentist's obituary" Honorable Mention, 2006 Brady Senryu Contest, *Frogpond*, 30:1, Winter 2007. "rushing stream" Runner-up, Contemporary Category, Haiku Now Contest, 2011, *Carving Darkness: 2011 Red Moon Anthology*. Jim Ka-cian et al, editors. Winchester, Virginia: Red Moon Press, 2012.

Tanya McDonald: "top of the space needle" "Per Diem" blog, May 2012, Haiku Foundation. "fresh gingerbread" *Modern Haiku* 42:1 Spring 2011. "log truck" *Bottle Rockets* #24 (12:2), 2011.

Margaret D. McGee: "slow, slow dusk" *Heron's Nest* 11:2, June 2009. "the doctor says" *Heron's Nest* 13:1, March 2011. "can't be helped" *Modern Haiku* 42:2, Summer 2011.

anne mckay: "pale fingers" and "the pears we waited for" *A cappella: Selected and New Poems*, Vancouver, British Columbia: Cacanadadada Press, 1994.

Mary Fran Meer: "a spent leaf" *Unbroken Curve*, Portland, Oregon: North-west Region, Haiku Society of America, 1996. "son's fluting whistle" Honorable Mention, Washington Poets Association Haiku Contest, 1994; *Wooing the Meadowlark*, Bellevue, Washington: Miraclear Press, 1997. "on the back road" *Brussels Sprout* XII:1, January 1995.

Mas Odoi: "hope for world peace" *On Crimson Wings*, Centennial An-thology of the Japanese Consulate of Seattle, Redmond, Washington: Laughing CyPress, 2001.

John L. Platt: "Lily pads float" *When Butterflies Come*, Haiku Society of America Members' Anthology, 1993. "Lilacs swaying" *Echoes Across the Cascades*, Bellevue, Washington: Northwest Region of the Haiku Society of America, 1994.

Francine Porad: "poolside, we chat" *Point Judith Light*, 2:1, March 1993; Itoen Tea Contest Winner, 1996; *Ladles and Jellyspoons: Presentations*, Mercer Island, Washington: Vandina Press, 1996. "vacation's end" *The Patchwork Quilt*, Mercer Island, Washington: Vandina Press, 1993. "birdhouse empty of seed" Heron's Nest Award, *Heron's Nest* 5:4, April 2003. "open house" *Joy Is My Middle Name*, Mercer Island, Washington: Vandina Press, 1993.

Ce Rosenow: "last rays of sunlight" *Bashō Festival Dedicatory Anthology* 48, Ueno City, Japan: Bashō Museum, 1994. "starry night" *North Lake*, Hillsboro, Oregon: Mountain Gate Press, 2004. "the water's surface" *Woodnotes* 5, Spring 1990.

Helen Russell: "he tells me the word" *Heron's Nest* 11:4, December 2009. "a cloud across the sun" *Distant Sounds*, privately published, 2008.

Marilyn Sandall: "morning mist" *Standing Still*, Haiku North America Conference Anthology, Michael Dylan Welch and Ruth Yarrow editors, Sammamish, Washington: Press Here, 2011. "nest hole" *Flower of Another Country: 2007 Members' Anthology*, Wanda D. Cook and Linda Porter, editors, Hadley, Massachusetts: Haiku Society of America, 2007.

Michelle Schaefer: "tennis backspin" *Modern Haiku* 44:1, Winter–Spring 2013. "hospital window" *Daily Haiku*, February 25, 2012. "the big dipper" Honorable Mention, 2011 Henderson Haiku Contest, *Frogpond* 35:1, Winter 2012.

Judt Shrode: "alone" Vancouver Cherry Blossom Festival Sakura Award, 2008.

Sarah Singer: "After the blind" Editors' Choice Award, *Brussels Sprout* IX: 2, May 1992. "Wind a muted horn" *Brussels Sprout* IX: 3, September 1992.

Carmi Soifer: "they bloom again" *Modern Haiku* 43:2, Summer 2012. "the shell's story" Second Place, 2010 Francine Porad Contest; *Cascade*, Washington Poets Association, 2011. "May rain" *Heron's Nest*, XIII:1, March 2011.

Sheila Sondik: "virginia rail" *Mu* #2, July 2011. "eroded sandstone" and "airplane window" *A Hundred Gourds* 1:1, December 2011. "The Blue Briefcase" *A Hundred Gourds* 1:4, Autumn 2012.

Ann Spiers: "a fist full" *Acorn* June 2011. "a thousand cuts" *Frogpond* 32:3, Fall 2009. "insects molting" *Roadrunner* 10:3, October 2010.

Carmen Sterba: "lapping shore water" *Frogpond* 33:1, Winter 2010, Museum of Haiku Literature Award. "sound of sweeping" *The Moss at Tokeiji*, Santa Fe, New Mexico: Deep North Press, 2010.

Dean Summers: "pitch black" *Cicada* 21, 1995. "before dawn" *Frogpond* 26:2 [Summer] 2003.

M. Anne Sweet: "Listening to Mozart" *Brussels Sprout* VI:3, September 1989.

Angela Terry: "trying to name" Honorable Mention, 2011 Robert Spiess Memorial Haiku Award; *Modern Haiku* 42:2, Summer 2011. "fast flowing river" *Frogpond* 35:2, Spring/Summer 2012. "our power" *Notes from the Gean*, June 2012.

Kathleen Tice: "white oleanders" *Familiar & Foreign: Haiku & Linked Verse*, Richard Tice with Jack Lyon et al, West Valley, Utah: Waking Lion Press, 2008.

Richard Tice: "moving together" *Cicada* 4:3, 1980. "Lightning" *Station Stop*, Salt Lake City: Middlewood Press, 1986. "more than yesterday" *Kō*, Spring–Summer 1997.

Eve Triem: "In the tasseling" *Brussels Sprout* VII:3, September 1990. "Two birds eat and eat" from "Haiku in America" essay manuscript, date unknown.

Billie Wilson: "no wind today" Editors' Choice, *Heron's Nest* VI:3, 2004; Special Mention, *The Heron's Nest Sixth Annual Valentine Awards* (2005). "the trail narrows" *Tempes Libre/Free Times*, October 2011; "Per Diem" blog, May 2012, Haiku Foundation."Shades of Blue" *Frogpond* 29:2, Spring/Summer 2006.

Brad Wolthers: "summit" Haiku In English column, *Mainichi Daily News*, Tokyo, Japan, 1989. "old barn roof" *Sand, Stone, and Other Living Things*, Eugene, Oregon: Mountains & River Press, 2011.

Ruth Yarrow: "gull overhead" First Place, 2011 Haiku North America Conference Kukai.

Cindy Zackowitz: "daylight moon" *Heron's Nest* 12:3, September 2010. "woodpecker" *Frogpond* 22:3, [Autumn] 1999.

INDEX OF CONTRIBUTORS

Made in the USA
Charleston, SC
09 June 2014